DONNAKARAN

NEWYORK

First published in the United States of America in 1998
by UNIVERSE PUBLISHING
A Division of Rizzoli International Publications, Inc.
300 Park Avenue South
New York, NY 10010

and

THE VENDOME PRESS

ISBN: 0-7893-0203-9

Printed and bound in France

Library of Congress Catalog Card Number: 98-60240

UNIVERSE OF FASHION

DONNAKARAN
NEWYORK

UNIVERSE / VENDOME

Foreword

"In 1985, when I started Donna Karan New York,
I set out to design modern clothes for modern people.
Today that is still my mission.
I'm inspired by the artist that lies in all of us.
A sense of character. Individuality. Creativity.
The soul that learns from the past.
The spirit that anticipates the future.
The body that is alive with sensuality.
And the heart that knows no bounds.
That's why for me, expression lies in simplicity.
Why black forms the perfect canvas.
And a tactile caress has such sensual power.
Design must be flexible—a chameleon, an exploration.
Because modern souls don't stand still.
They keep moving forward, evolving, creating.
Forever inspired by life."

Donna Karan

Interview with Donna Karan by Ingrid Sischy

Ingrid Sischy: As I understand it, a pivotal moment for you as a designer was in 1974, coming at exactly the same time as another monumental event in your life, the birth of your daughter, Gabby, right?

Donna Karan: Yes. I was at Anne Klein, where I had already been working on and off for about six years. I was pregnant, and went into labor at work, right there at the Anne Klein offices. The baby was ten days late, and the pressure was on for the Fall preview collection. This was in the days when they still showed what was known back then as "capsule collections." Basically, Anne and I did everything, period. But she was in the hospital. And when I also went to the hospital to give birth, there was nobody to finish the collection.

Sischy: Had you known how sick Anne Klein was?

Karan: No. She had cancer. In those days, nobody knew you had it, or talked about it. It was not discussed.

Sischy: Keep going.

Karan: Well, the office kept calling to ask when I was coming back. I remember needing to say, "Would you like to know whether I had a boy or a girl?" Anyway, I asked the doctor about going back to work, and he said, "What about the stitches?" I replied, "Don't worry about the stitches. There are plenty of seamstresses in the office."

Sischy: [laughs] He must have known there was no stopping that situation.

Karan: Well, what he did offer is that I could return to work in a week. So, I went home, to a brand-new house in Long Island. There wasn't a stick of furniture, but we wanted to have the reception for the baby at home. So, here we are in the new house in Long Island, with a new baby. The table's made, the lox and the bagels are out, the guests are on their way, and the next thing that happens is that trucks are pulling up to the driveway. And then racks with clothes, and half-made clothes, come pouring into the house. Next, everybody from the office comes inside the house, and they're even bringing the dummies and the fitting models with them.

Sischy: [laughs] Only in the fashion world!

Karan: The phone rings. Somebody answers it. We're told that Anne Klein has died.

Sischy: You must have been devastated. She meant so much to you.

Karan: I felt very alone. I called up her husband, and he said, "Anne would have liked you to finish the collection. I know her, and that's what she would have wanted."

Sischy: And you were pretty much instantly named as her successor. After a while, your friend from Parsons, Louis Dell'Olio, joined you as designer, but what a way to have it all fall on your shoulders!

Karan: Yes. I didn't even know what hit me. Anne was gone. I had just had the baby. And right before that, I had told them that I wasn't going to continue working. I had planned to stay home and be a mother. It wasn't that I didn't want to be a designer. I just wanted the experience of being home with my child. I grew up with a working mother. And it's tough. Talk about what you resist, persists!

Sischy: What did your mother do?

Karan: She was in the fashion industry. So was my father.

Sischy: So, fashion was, in fact, in your blood.

Karan: My mother was a showroom model, and then she became a sales person. They called her Queenie. Basically, I grew up on Seventh Avenue. My father made custom-made suits.

Sischy: So, it all fits, huh?

Karan: Yes. I had to get to the point where I realized that. But now, I really do believe that it was written.

Sischy: I note that in the official chronology of your life, it says quite proudly that when you were first hired at Anne Klein in 1969, you were fired.

Karan: [laughs] Right.

Sischy: How did you get there in the first place?

Karan: Well, I wanted a summer job. So they hired me, and convinced me not to go back to Parsons, where I was at school. Then I got fired nine months later—after I'd quit school for them. It was awful. Anne herself didn't fire me. The assistant to the assistant to the assistant fired me, or something like that. But then I ended up working for another woman who was brilliant, Patty Cappalli. The name of that company was Addenda. She took me to Europe.

Sischy: And how did it turn out that you ended up back at Anne Klein, the scene of the crime?

Karan: Well, the woman that originally fired me either got fired or left. I can't remember. But when they offered me another job I said, I'd really like to have not my old job back, but the next level up of my job.

Sischy: And clearly, the destiny between you and Anne Klein wasn't over because at that point you joined the company as Associate Designer. This was in 1971 and within a short amount of time, you were basically responsible for the collections. What do you think it was about you that made Anne Klein put you in a position where everyone was depending on you so much?

Karan: That's just the way it was. There wasn't a staff. There weren't specialists. One did it all. That's how we learned. I feel badly today that a lot of people don't have the opportunity that I had in terms of true learning. For instance, I went to all the fabric shows. That was my way of life. We really explored the European market in terms of fabrics and textiles, and all that. I had no connections. I never knew where I was going or what I was doing, I was just learning on my feet.

Sischy: Your first collection as head of Anne Klein was a smash hit, accompanied by the headline, "A Star is Born," right?

Karan: Yes. That was very, very sweet.

Sischy: You're being modest. In fact, you really kept Anne Klein on the map, and hauled in plenty of awards for it! By the time you launched your own company with your husband, Stephan Weiss, in 1985, Donna Karan New York, you were already a legend.

How did you know it was the perfect time to leave Anne Klein and start Donna Karan?

Karan: You have to know when something is ready to be born. If you try to do everything within the same entity, it doesn't work. What I wanted to do was design clothes for my friends and for myself. I wanted to make a little collection that was all about need and desire. Being a designer led me to the questions in life that I constantly have—the questions that I have to explore. What do I need? What do I desire? What do I hope for? Originally, I wanted simple, comfort clothes for me and my friends, such as a few black pieces.

Sischy: Female friends?

Karan: Yes. When I say "my friends," I mean it literally and metaphorically. I mean women who, like myself, live a hectic life, who are in touch with their own sensuality, who know their own bodies, who know what they want. I was frustrated by what I saw was mostly available to women.

Sischy: It sounds like a simple thing, but in fact, clothes that were actually sensitive to what women truly felt—instead of mostly being about what people thought women should wear—were practically revolutionary. Your idea started the way lots of new things start—with a dissatisfaction with what you were seeing around you.

Karan: It seemed like there was no bridge between sportswear and citywear. To me the woman was left out most of the time. The only American who had been exploring that territory was Halston. He'd had a modernity that was unique. He'd understood comfort clothes, and real ease, in a simple, sexy kind of way. Halston had expressed the possibilities of jersey. For me it was, and is, about cashmere.

11

Sischy: Did you sense that lots of women were frustrated that they didn't have many options?

Karan: There weren't any as far as I was concerned! I was looking for hosiery. I was looking for underwear. I was looking for a pair of shoes. I was looking for a bag, a belt. It wasn't just about the clothes. That's why I was so frustrated. I wanted a sense of feel and touch. I wanted to create direct contact between myself and the consumer. That was my dream: I wanted to talk to women—woman to woman. That evolved to wanting to talk directly to men, too. Men haven't been taken into consideration any more than women have been. For the most part, the whole issue of men's clothes has been reduced to either two buttons, or three buttons, or four buttons. Why can't a man wear his clothes separately the way a woman does? Why does it have to be about his suits, and then his sports-wear? With men, first you go to the suit department, then you go to the sweater department, then you go to the shirts, you know, the system. Why does it have to be this way?

Sischy: The thing that was said almost immediately about you was how much you understood women emotionally.

Karan: Hey, I live the same tortured life that every other woman does when I look in the mirror. What woman does not stand in front of that mirror and say, "I gotta go here. What am I going to wear? Look at my body!" I don't care whether she's skinny, or whether her ankles are this or her knees are that, one's confrontation with oneself is difficult.

Sischy: I know people whom you've fitted, and they always comment on how you make them feel less self-conscious and feel less alone in their insecurities. They say that instead of the usual intimidating experience, clothes with you become a comfortable process. And they are always struck by how real you are. To me, this is one reason why you've been so successful—you make people feel understood and heard.

Karan: We're all human beings. And I don't want to pretend to be something that I'm not. I think that's something that people have gravitated to, and can identify with. People want to feel good. Growing up I resented the looks that were imposed on people. I was allowed girlie-girlie stuff. And I wanted very simple clothes—even then it was black clothes and sweaters, you know.

Sischy: And finally, in 1985, you launched your own collection: Donna Karan New York.

Karan: Yes. It started thirteen years ago in my apartment, in the front bedroom. We had pin holes all over our walls.

Sischy: Now you have sixteen Donna Karan stores worldwide, and forty DKNY stores, right? And that's not including your line D, the home collections, the hosiery, the beauty products, the fragrances, the shoes, the furniture, and on it goes. Not bad for just over twelve years' work.

Karan: When we began, it was my husband, Stephan, myself, and then I hired our first employee, Alida Miller. Then, Patti Cohen came. Eventually, we moved to 40 West 40th Street, where there was a little apartment with a little kitchen. This felt like a big expansion.

Sischy: Now you have a big presence on and around Seventh Avenue and you're considered one of the companies who make Seventh Avenue what it is—which is a street that is synonymous with fashion. And even though you're very much an international company, you're also a New York institution. Tell me about the evolution of the connection between your name and the city of New York. It seems so right, not just because you're such a New Yorker, but because of everything you stand for, in both your life and your work: freedom, a forward-looking philosophy, selfhood, self-realization, creative energy, et cetera. For instance, think about that campaign you did about a woman, wearing Donna Karan, running for President of the United States of America. That take-charge, new-world attitude is exactly what I'm talking about. So, tell me how you decided to actually directly link your name to the city that has always stood for the future, for dreams, and for making something of oneself.

Karan: I never wanted the company to simply be called Donna Karan. One of Patti Cohen's early jobs was to help us find what our logo was going to be. Patti found Peter Arnell. And that led to the New York story. Patti kept saying, "I want you to meet this guy, Peter Arnell, to work with us on our creative. I think you'll like him." And I did. Meanwhile, I'm sitting in my kitchen, and I see this Maud Frizon shoe box. It says Maud Frizon Paris–New York. I say, "That's it!" Then people started asking, "Well, what about the folks in California?" And we told them, "Everybody wants a piece of New York. New York is the hub. New York is international. New York is the bridge. New York means being international. And that's how Donna Karan New York was named. And then from there, it was natural to go to DKNY.

Sischy: And boom! With your first collection, you had what appeared to be instant success. Clearly, it wasn't instantaneous, but was rather a product of years of thought and experience and evolution.

Karan: I have to say that I could not have done anything like this without my husband, Stephan. He dealt with all the legal work; he dealt with all the negotiations. He formed the company. He left me free to design. There would have been no company had my husband not made this incredible contribution.

Sischy: To me, the fact that your husband is an artist with strong conceptual interests always meant that you had another person who you totally trusted, who had a different way of looking at things, who was pulling with you. With Stephan, you had a partner who was also willing on the dream, and naming the dream, and dreaming with you. I can imagine just how supportive that was because I know both of you. And I know your respect for creativity, Donna. So I can guess how much it meant.

Karan: You are right about my belief in creativity, and in creative people. That's partly how I get satisfaction—supporting creativity. It's not necessarily about my creativity, but about putting the creativity of everyone together, and supporting creativity on many levels. I'm happy to be a catalyst for creativity. There have been, and continue to be, many creative people whom I have the honor of working with—and you are right about the role of my husband in all this. He is one of those who constantly challenge me to go places I don't want to travel.

Sischy: But you seem to have always been working towards a larger vision of what fashion could be in people's lives.

Karan: Well, our vision was very clear from the very beginning. It was never exclusively about clothes; we never wanted it to be simply about fashion. It was always meant to be about everything that touches a person's senses, starting with the sense of touch.

Sischy: And you've always seemed to have had certain missions.

Karan: Yes. For example, I had a mission to take ties off of men. And why can't a woman go out in a T-shirt? The bodysuit that I did is basically a T-shirt. It was about giving women back their bodies and giving them back the comfort of their bodies.

Sischy: Did you always like working with the customer so much?

Karan: I always understood it. It was what I knew best. When I was fourteen, I worked in a clothing store—Sherrie's, they called it. And I was the best salesgirl.

Sischy: Now you want to combine the market with the soul.

Karan: To me, if the artist's hand is lost, you might as well throw away the key. The minute it becomes bottom line, you're no longer in it.

Sischy: Some people say that designers shouldn't think this way.

Karan: I don't think I could survive as a designer today if I didn't think this way. It's my water; it's my breath; it's my air; it's my essence. It's about what I react to, what inspires me, what my emotion is. For me, fashion is about touch, and feel, and emotion. And it should heighten your senses on every level. For Spring/Summer 1998, I was obsessed with creating the light of the bay that I had been experiencing. I would look at the rocks, and look at the bay, the light, the glass, the light in the sky, and ask, HOW do I communicate that sky color, that water color, that glass color? You have to understand why something means something to you. And in fashion these things are never finished. They just continue. In this field, you're always solving the problems. Even after a collection, it's not the end. It's always a beginning—the next collection. It's always the beginning of what you're about to say, because the creative process in fashion is so continual. It never stops. And it shouldn't. You never feel like you've finally said it. That's why I always like to write on my releases, "To Be Continued." And I consider the customer a part of my creative process. I need the customer as part of the dialogue that has to go on. I'm always listening to my friends saying, "Why can't I find this? Why can't I find that?"

Sischy: Did you used to shop a lot?

Karan: No.

Sischy: Why? Because it was so horrible?

Karan: In department stores? I hated the experience. Flea markets? Love, love.

Sischy: And when you would have to go and buy clothes—

Karan: Forget it. That's why I became a designer! I couldn't stand it! It was so painful! I hated shopping. Going into a dressing room for me was like the kiss of death. And I know a lot of people have this problem. So, today, I want to create places where people get what they want. I don't want to confuse them. I want a woman or a man to be able to walk into one of my environments and feel taken care of. I want them to walk in and communicate, and feel communicated with. I want to create that kind of retail environment—places that are compelling to go into. I'm going to do that more and more in the future—create places and things so that people can feel transformed, listened to, nurtured, taken care of, and special. There has to be something more to all this than just merchandise.

17

NEW YORK

$2.95 • MAY 6,

DONNA KARAN
CORPORATE GODDESS

THE MOST SUCCESSFUL WOMAN ON SEVENTH AVENUE HAS GONE NEW AGE, AND NOW SHE'S GOING PUBLIC. WILL WALL STREET LOVE DONNA AS MUCH AS HER CUSTOMERS DO? BY REBECCA MEAD

New York Times Magazine

MAY 4, 1986 / SECTION 6

ESIGNER DONNA KARAN

How a
Fashion Star
Is Born

BY CARRIE DONOVAN

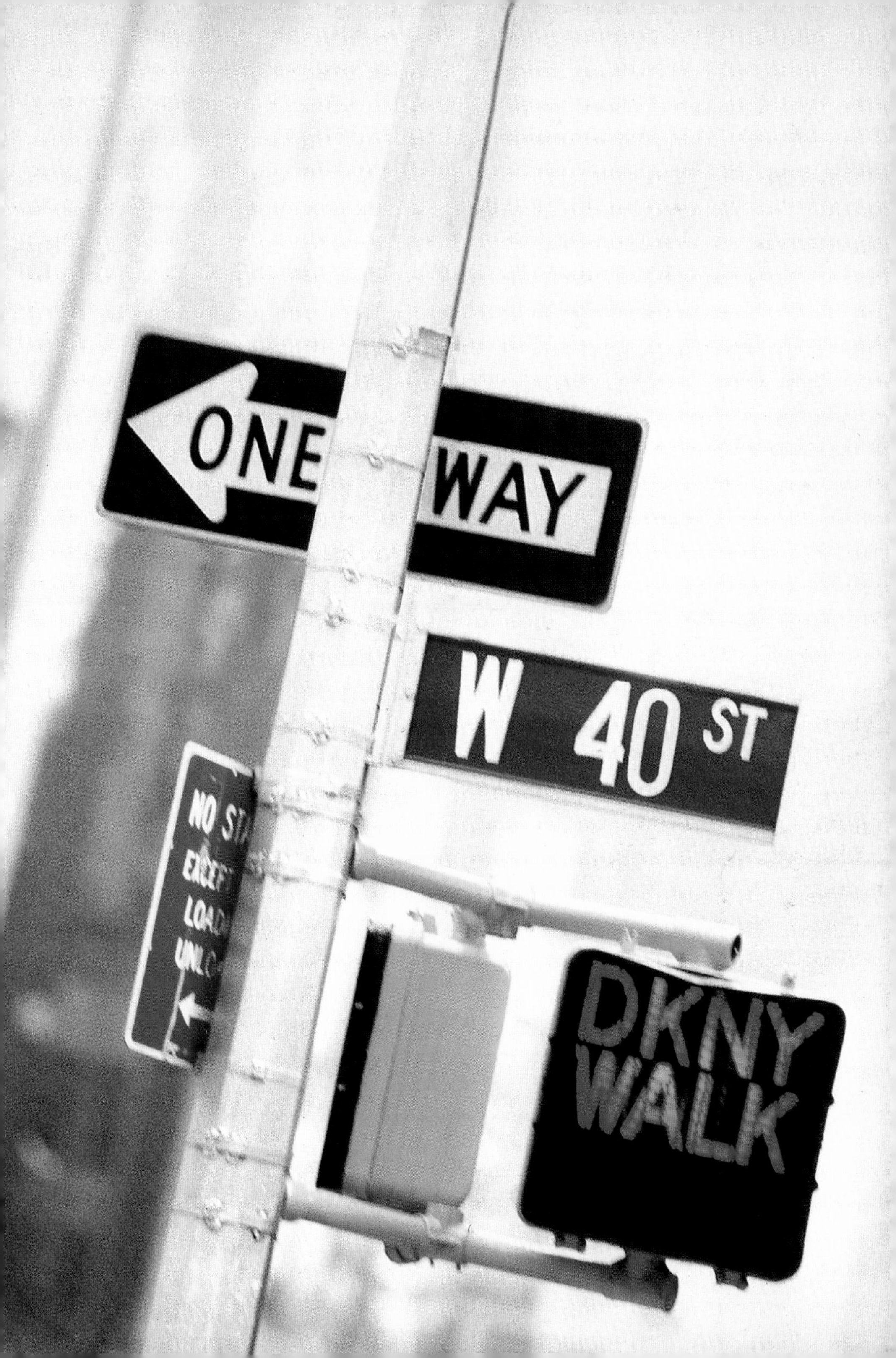
ONE WAY
W 40 ST
DKNY
WALK

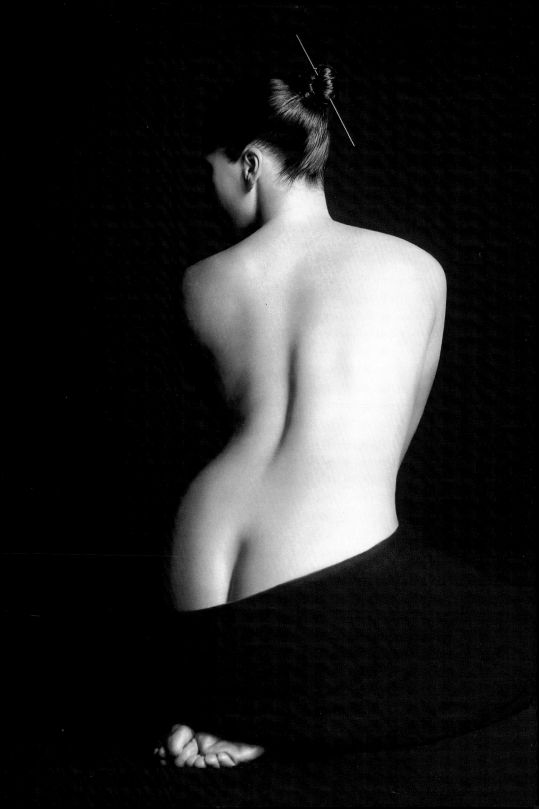

Chronology

1948   Born Donna Faske to Gabrielle and Helen Faske in Long Island, NY

1968–69   Attends Parsons School of Design
A summer job at Anne Klein & Co. becomes a permanent position

1970   Marriage to Mark Karan

1971   Named associate designer at Anne Klein

1974–75   Daughter born, Gabrielle Karan
Anne Klein dies, Karan named successor
Louis Dell'Olio, a friend from Parsons, joins Karan to design Anne Klein

1977   Wins first Coty Award, highest American fashion honor of the time

1981   Wins second Coty Award

1982–83   Marriage to Stephan Weiss

1984   Wins third Coty Award and is elected to Coty Hall of Fame

1985   Launch of Donna Karan New York: the Fall collection debuts with head to toe collection including accessories and jewelry
Named Designer of the Year by the Council of Fashion Designers (CFDA)

1987   Debut of Donna Karan Hosiery, licensed with Hanes Hosiery
Hosiery advertising campaign wins CFDA award

1988   Launch of DKNY, clothing inspired by the spirit and energy of New York
Debut of Donna Karan Eyewear

1990   Named Designer of the Year by the CFDA for the second time
Initiates and co-chairs "Seventh on Sale," raising $7 million to benefit Aids charities

1992   The Donna Karan Beauty Company debuts with signature fragrance
Donna Karan Menswear debuts
Donna Karan Shoes, Intimates debuts
Named Menswear Designer of the Year by the CFDA

1993   DKNY Men's debuts
Milan office opens
Hosts benefit for Pediatric Aids with Elizabeth Glazer, which becomes an annual event

Carrie Otis for The Donna Karan Beauty Company, 1996. © Photo: Herb Ritts.

| 1994 | DKNY flagship store opens in London |
| | Publishes book *DKNY:NYC* |

1995	Publishes book *Modern Souls*
	First issue of *Woman to Woman*, Karan's editorial communication with her customer
	Designs costumes for Martha Graham's production "Snow on the Mesa"

1996	Donna Karan International goes public on the New York Stock Exchange
	Donna Karan New York flagship store opens in London
	Participates in the Biennale di Firenze

1997	Named Designer of the Year by the CFDA for the third time
	Signature Donna Karan debuts
	Donna Karan home accessories collection debuts
	D by DKNY debuts
	Publishes book *Leg*; proceeds benefit Gilda's Club
	There are sixteen Donna Karan New York stores worldwide
	There are forty-seven DKNY stores worldwide

Rosemary McGrotha wearing Donna Karan New York. Fall 1986 campaign. © Photo: Denis Piel.

Donna Karan

Karan and daughter Gabby Karan "Having a child is the most creative thing you can do. Gabby is my best friend, my greatest achievement ever." *Vogue*, 1996. © Photo: Annie Leibovitz.

In Women We Trust A presidential advertising campaign with a feminine spin in pinstripes and pearls. Spring 1992 campaign with Rosemary McGrotha. © Photo: Peter Lindbergh.

Public Persona Eleven years after opening, Karan's company went from privately held to publicly traded. Photo: Jesse Frohman. © *New York Magazine* (May 6, 1996).
The Jet Set From its conception, Karan's designs appealed to the high-powered woman on the go. Fall 1986 campaign. © Photo: Denis Piel.

Luxurious Chaos In Karan's world, a woman's many roles—mother, wife, executive—are all part of the modern mix of life. Fall 1986 campaign. © Photo: Denis Piel.

Modern Souls "I set out to design modern clothes for modern people. Today, that is still my mission," says Karan. From the tenth anniversary campaign, "Modern Souls," Fall 1995. Fred Ward in stretch tweed and Kristen McMenamy in camel and satin. © Photos: Herb Ritts.

Woman to Woman Karan, the consummate communicator. Photo: Gus Van Sant. © *Harper's Bazaar*, 1997.
Biennale di Firenze Karan participated in the first exhibition. Her site, held at the historic chapel Museo del Bigallo, featured three velvet gowns suspended from the vaulted ceiling. © Photo: Editions Assouline, 1997.

Natural Sophistication Actress Isabella Rossellini, a favorite muse, epitomizes the international, ageless woman for whom Karan designs. Here she wears DK's black leather jacket and crepe pants. © Photo: Steven Meisel, 1994.

System of Dressing Karan designs in systems, where flexible pieces, like those sampled here, work together to create a complete wardrobe. *Vogue*, 1995. © Photo: Steven Meisel, courtesy The Condé Nast Publications Ltd.

Strong, creative women inspire Karan, such as international author Benedetta Barzini (left), here wearing a doublefaced cashmere clutch, and actress Anouk Aimé (right), pictured in a tailored jacket. Both from "Modern Souls" campaign, Fall 1995. © Photos: Herb Ritts.

Black. Stretch. Body-Conscious. All quintessential DK elements. Karan's designs possess an innate sensuality, whether ready-to-wear or intimate apparel, as pictured here. © Photo: Peter Arnell, 1992.

The Art of the Leg Karan's hosiery solves problems, be they of the body or fashion kind. Left: the Nudes introduced the illusion of bare perfection. Nadja Auermann models. © Photo: Herb Ritts, 1995. Right: black matte hosiery, the Karan innovation that started a hosiery revolution. © Photo: Peter Arnell, 1989.

Body Language Karan dramatically silhouettes the body through proportion and the contrast of skin and fabric, especially matte jersey and stretch crepe. Here, a sleek runway figure for Spring 1995. © Photo: Gerrado Samoza.

How a Fashion Star is Born *New York Times Magazine* cover story by Carrie Donovan. Photo: Chuck Baker. © *New York Times Magazine* (May 4, 1986).

The Artisan Touch Working with artists from around the world, Karan seeks the creative hand for its individuality, its one-of-a-kind luxury. Iman models a hand-beaded mesh dress for the Spring 1997 campaign. © Photo: Peter Lindbergh.

Objects of Desire The seduction of form, the embrace of fabric, the sensuality of expression. Karan photographed with four limited edition evening designs. German *Vogue*, 1997. © Photo: Arthur Elgort, courtesy The Condé Nast Publications Ltd.

Demi Moore and Bruce Willis "embody all that is modern," says Karan of the celebrated couple who starred in her Fall 1996 campaign. Left: Moore wears a navy stretch jersey and wool unitard. Right: Willis dons a black leather jacket, she a backless cashmere sweater. © Photos: Peter Lindbergh.

A Marriage of Art and Passion Karan with her husband, the sculptor Stephan Weiss. *Vanity Fair*, 1993. © Photo: Annie Leibovitz.

Cut from the Same Cloth Karan unites the soft with the strong, the feminine with the masculine. Linda Evangelista in menswear-inspired pants. Fall 1997 campaign. © Photo: Peter Lindbergh.
Portraits in Black Three variations on a theme in Karan's favorite color. Photo: Neil Kirk, 1996. © British *Vogue*/The Condé Nast Publications Ltd.

London Calling Karan's first global flagship Collection store opened on New Bond Street, London, 1996. © Photo: Chris Gascoigne/View Pictures.

New York State of Mind Karan's home town of New York City and all it represents remain her greatest source of inspiration. Left: from the men's and women's collections, Fall 1993. © Photo: Peter Lindbergh. Right: Queensboro Bridge. © Photo: Peter Arnell, 1990.

DKNY The fast-paced, accessible, street side of Donna Karan New York, introduced in 1989. © Illustration: Peter Arnell.

Street Signs. DKNY embraces all things New York—its spirit, its energy, its mix of cultures. Left: a wet, exuberant study in black on Beri Smither. Right: a fashionable intersection. Fall 1994 campaign. © Photos: Peter Lindbergh.

An Environmental Palette DKNY colors and textures are often lifted from the street. Left: a sea of yellow taxicabs. © Photo: Peter Lindbergh. Right: the slickness of wet pavement captured in rainboots. Fall 1994 campaign. © Photo: Franz Walderdorff.

Scenes from New York From high above to far below. Left: an aerial view of the NYC skyline. Right: standing in the subway, Beri Smither wears the uniform of the city, a black leather jacket. Fall 1994 campaign. © Photos: Peter Lindbergh.

DKNY Goes Hollywood From real life to real glam. Left: Mark Vanderloo and DKNY Men's matinée appeal. Right: Shalom takes a break in a sharskin short trench. Spring 1995 campaign. © Photos: Peter Lindbergh.

Universal Language of Style Speaking to every generation, DKNY has labels extending to men, women and children. Here, a DKNY family, from left to right: Mark Leka, Peter Fortier and Rosemary McGrotha. Spring 1993 campaign. © Photo: Denis Piel.

Freedom of Expression DKNY advances personal style with flexible, lifestyle pieces that become one with the wearer. Left: a view of the Statue of Liberty. Right: Beri Smither wearing the classic trench on the Brooklyn Bridge. Fall 1994 campaign. © Photos: Peter Lindbergh.

DKNY Jeans, introduced in 1992, embraces a lifestyle that is friendly, real and wearable. Rosemary gets comfortable: left, nubuck fringed jacket, Spring 1992. © Photo: Peter Lindbergh. Right, denim on denim with white camisole, Spring 1990. © Photo: Peter Arnell.

The Heart of New York They met on this DKNY shoot and now real-life couple Esther Cañadas and Mark Vanderloo are the official faces of the brand. Says Karan, "I see our campaigns as slices of life, capturing their relationship and lives unfolding in photos." Fall 1997 campaign. © Photo: Peter Lindbergh.

Acknowledgments

The publishers would like to thank Donna Karan New York, particularly Dee Salomon, Patti Cohen and Catherine Barton, as well as Emily Anderson, Stacey Berger, Kathleen Boyes, Chris Carswell, Ray Dipetro, Hans Dorsinville, Nicole Franchuk, Monica Kim, Trey Laird, Letisha Marrero, Sarah Muñoz, Christine Notaro and Jill Schaaf, for their invaluable assistance in producing this book.

Many thanks also to the photographers Peter Lindbergh, Herb Ritts, Neil Kirk, Marc Hispard, Arthur Elgort, Steven Meisel, Peter Arnell, Denis Piel, Chris Gascoigne, Franz Walderdorff, Annie Leibovitz, Jesse Frohman and Chuck Baker.

Finally this book could not have been published without the help and co-operation of Sandrine Bizzard (Michele Filomeno), Sabine Killinger (Elite), Alexandre de la Patellière, Alexandre Percy (Outline-Acte 2), Michelle Ocampo (Arthur Elgort), Ruth Eagleton (Condé Nast Publications), Michèle Zaquin (Les Publications Condé Nast), Gayle Mault (View Pictures), Brian Bennett (Lamprecht & Bennett Inc.), Vernon Jolly, Rosanna Sguera (Art & Commerce), Jean-Bernard (Contact Press Images) and Barbara (Arnell Group).